OPUS 5

Progression in Music 11–14

Rob Blythe
Derek Hobbs

Editor: Chris Harrison

Heinemann Educational Publishers
Halley Court, Jordan Hill, Oxford OX2 8EJ
Part of Harcourt Education

Heinemann is the registered trademark of Harcourt Education Limited

Text © Harcourt Education Limited 2007

Units 1, 3, 4, 5 and 6 written by Rob Blythe
Unit 2 written by Derek Hobbs

First published 2007

12 11 10 09 08 07

10 9 8 7 6 5 4 3 2 1

British Library Cataloguing in Publication Data is available from the British Library on request.

ISBN 978 0 435812 50 8

Copyright notice

Produced by Artistix

Original illustrations © Harcourt Education Limited 2007

Picture research by Liz Alexander

Cover photo/illustration © Getty

Printed and bound at Scotprint, Haddington, East Lothian

Acknowledgements

The author and publisher would like to thank the following individuals and organisations for permission to reproduce photographs:

ArenaPAL/Boosey and Hawkes p.58; ARS, NY and DACS, London 2007/Tate Images p.44; Corbis p.53 (left); Corbis/Bettman p.56; Corbis/Fabrice Coffrini p.14; Corbis/James Marshall p.36; Corbis/Underwood and Underwood p.9; C.R.A. Davies p.29; DKImages p.33; EMI Music p.42 (CD cover); Harcourt Education/Trevor Clifford, Hertfordshire Country Music Service p.30; Harcourt Education/Trevor Clifford, Wembley Drum Centre p.32; Lebrecht Music & Arts p.25; Lebrecht /Jonathan Evant p.41 (bottom); Lebrecht/R Booth p.50; Redferns/DEL003_Robert_JOHNSON 3958 p.5; Redferns/Jeremy Butler p.48; Redferns/Keith Bernstein p.60; Redferns/Odile Noel p.47; Rex Features/Everett Collection p.42; Rex Features/ITV p.34; Rex Features/Nils Jorgensen p.46; Ronald Grant Archive p.11; Redferns/Henrietta Butler p.41 (top); ©Tate London, ARS, NY and DACS, London 2007 p.40; World Religions Photo Library/M Forsyth p.53 (right).

The authors and publishers would like to thank the following for permission to reproduce printed copyright material:

In The Mood (pages 6 and 8)
Words by Andy Razaf
Music by Joe Garland
© 1939 Shapiro Bernstein & Co Inc, USA
Peter Maurice Music Co Ltd, London WC2H 0QY
Reproduced by permission of International Music Publications Ltd (a trading name of Faber Music Ltd)
All Rights Reserved.

And All That Jazz (page 12)
Words by Fred Ebb
Music by John Kander
© 1973 Kander and Ebb Inc and Unichappell Music Inc, USA
Warner/Chappell North America Ltd, London W6 8BS
Reproduced by permission of Faber Music Ltd
All Rights Reserved.

Tubular Bells (page 43)
Words and Music by Mike Oldfield
© 1973 EMI Virgin Music Ltd, London WC2H 0QY
Reproduced by permission of International Music Publications Ltd (a trading name of Faber Music Ltd)
All Rights Reserved.

Stand By Me (page 61)
Words and Music by Jerry Leiber, Mike Stoller and Ben E. King.
© 1961 (Renewed) JERRY LEIBER MUSIC, MIKE STOLLER MUSIC and TRIO MUSIC COMPANY.
All Rights Reserved.

Every effort has been made to contact copyright holders of material reproduced in this book. Any omissions will be rectified in subsequent printings if notice is given to the publishers.

Contents

Chords into jazz

In this unit you will:

- learn about different types of chords and how these are used in jazz
- learn how chords can be put together to form a chord progression
- learn how melodies are performed in jazz
- learn how improvisation is used in jazz
- learn how jazz chords have been used in music of different times and places

by:

- listening to, performing and composing using a range of different types of chords from jazz music
- performing a well-known jazz chord progression called the 12-bar blues and a walking bass line
- performing a melody that is based on notes taken from a chord progression in a traditional swing jazz style
- improvising over a chord progression using notes of the blues scale
- exploring how chords in jazz have been used in a modern song written for the stage

because:

- it will help you to understand more about how different chords are constructed and used to create different effects and textures
- the 12-bar blues is a famous chord progression that forms the structure of all blues music and much more
- jazz melodies were often not written down exactly as performed
- improvisation is a key feature of jazz and many other styles of music
- many jazz musicians improvise melodies using notes of the blues scale and notes from the chords of the music
- chords form the basic harmony of a piece of music not only in jazz but also in many different types and styles of music.

Feelin' blue in just three chords

In this lesson you will:

- learn to play the 12-bar blues chord progression

- listen to and perform a walking bass line.

Listening

1 To remind you what jazz music sounds like, you will be played three different pieces of jazz music.

   a Describe (in your own words) what you can hear. Think about the rhythm, texture and structure.

   b Discuss your answers with the rest of the class. What conclusions can you reach about each piece?

How does jazz music use chords?

Chords are the foundation of all jazz music. Jazz composers and musicians use many different types of chords to give their music different flavours. The three most important chords that you are going to learn to play are found in a type of music called the **blues**. The blues in its present form originated around 1900 among the black inhabitants of the southern USA.

The blues singer, Robert Johnson

Performing

2 Most blues music is based on a **chord sequence** called the **12-bar blues**. It is called this because the length of each verse of a blues song is twelve bars.

   a First, play the chords of C, G and F as shown below.

Chord of C   G E C   Chord of F   C A F   Chord of G   D B G

   b Use these chords to play the 12-bar blues chord sequence below. Remember to hold each of the chords for four beats. Alternatively, if you are able to, play each chord as four crotchets. Remember to play steadily and smoothly. The blues was not meant to be fast!

C – – –	C – – –	C – – –	C – – –
F – – –	F – – –	C – – –	C – – –
G – – –	F – – –	C – – –	C ♪♪♪

What is a walking bass line?

A **walking bass line** is frequently used in jazz and blues music.
It is called a walking bass line as it 'walks' up and down the
keyboard. You will learn to play the well-known walking bass
line from 'In The Mood' by Glenn Miller, a famous band leader
and composer.

Performing

3 Look at the first two bars of the walking bass line of the song 'In The Mood' by Glen Miller. It is based
on the chord of C, as in the first two bars of the 12-bar blues chord progression. Which two notes
have been 'added' to the chord?

C E G A B♭ A G E

Notation for the first two bars from the walking bass line of 'In the Mood'

Listening and performing

4 Listen to a version of 'In the Mood' and try to pick out the walking bass line. In pairs, you will now
learn the walking bass line to this song using the notation below.

   a Practise playing the notes in bold and count the other notes as rests.

   b When you are confident playing the bold notes, add in all the others to play the whole bass line.

Walking bass line for 'In the Mood'

Swinging the melody

In this lesson you will:

- learn about the boogie-woogie style of playing music
- learn how melodies are performed with a 'swing' in jazz and blues music
- perform the melody of 'In the Mood' in a swing style.

Boogie-woogie

Boogie-woogie is a style of blues piano playing that became very popular in the 1940s and was extended from piano to guitar, big band, and country and western music. It is characterised by a regular bass figure, a **riff** in the bass that elaborates on each chord while the right hand uses **trills** and melodic decoration. Sometimes, boogie-woogie is used to accompany singers and as a solo part in bands.

Playing with a swing

Much jazz and blues music is written like the riff shown in task 1. The musician tends to add the **swing** rhythm to it during performance.

Performing

1 Look at the riff below, which comes from a piece of boogie-woogie music. The **melody** is taken from notes of the blues scale (see page 9), while the bass part performs another riff.

In pairs, try playing the combined riff in two different ways:
- strictly as it is written
- in a swing style (your teacher will play it first to give you an idea).

A boogie-woogie riff

2 Look at the notes used in the first two bars of the melody line for 'In the Mood' shown below.

   a How do these compare with the chord used in the accompanying chord (page 5)?

   b Now follow the other notes used in the melody and see if you can work out how the melody has been composed using notes from the chords.

Melody line for 'In the Mood'

3 Now learn to play the melody part of 'In the Mood' above. Remember that you need to perform it in a 'swing' style, like the boogie-woogie riff you learnt for task 1. Once you can play the melody, work with a partner who can play the 12-bar blues walking bass line together with you.

Performing 'In the Mood'

In this lesson you will:

- learn how the blues scale is used in jazz improvisations and create your own improvisations using the blues scale

- learn to combine the features of jazz and chords to create a performance of a piece of jazz with improvisation sections and with a jazz style and feel to the music.

The blues scale

Many jazz musicians use the **blues scale** for their solo **improvisations**.
In the **key** of C, the notes of the blues scale are C, E♭, F, F#, G, B♭ and C:

C   E♭   F   F#   G   B♭   C

Performing

1 Look at the music example of the blues scale above, then practise playing the notes.

The Glenn Miller Band

The Glenn Miller Band

'In the Mood' was one of the Glenn Miller Band's most famous hits. This 'big band' played a type of jazz called swing which, like the blues, originated in America before becoming popular in the UK during World War II. Big bands such as the Glenn Miller Band comprised a large group of players, often more than 20, and played music in large dance halls and theatres.

Improvising on the blues scale

2 When you are all familiar with the scale, you will be asked, individually, to perform an eight-beat improvisation while the rest of the class plays the 12-bar blues chord sequence from lesson 1.1 (page 5). You will be invited to talk about others' improvisations (when everyone has performed) to discuss whose improvisations worked well and why.

Performing 'In the Mood'

3 Continue the work you started in task 3 of lesson 1.2 by putting together a jazz performance of 'In the Mood' to include some or all of the following elements:
- the 12-bar blues walking bass line
- the swing style melody
- the 12-bar blues chord progression
- jazz improvisations using the notes of the blues scale.

Try to swap round the roles in the performance so that both players get the opportunity to play all of the parts.

All that jazz!

In this lesson you will:

- learn how contemporary composers have used features of jazz in their music
- learn how 7th chords contrast in sound to other chords
- learn how chords are used in a modern jazz song written for the stage.

Chicago, the musical

The musical *Chicago* was first performed in New York on 3 June 1975. Set in downtown 1920s Chicago, it tells of murderesses Velma Kelly and Roxie Hart who find themselves on death row together and fight for the fame that will keep them from the gallows. As the tag line to the film version of this musical says: 'With the right song and dance, you can get away with murder.'

A still from *Chicago*

Constructing 7th chords

7th chords are often used in jazz music to create different musical effects. They are used in the song 'All That Jazz' from *Chicago*. They are constructed by taking the notes of a primary chord (in C, this would be C, E and G) and adding a note that is seven notes above the **root** (for the chord of C, the root will be C; seven notes above that is B). However, in jazz music we always need to flatten the seventh note by one semitone. So, the chord of C7 would be made up of C, E, G and B♭.

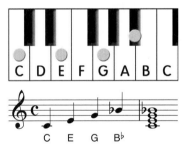

Listening to 'All That Jazz'

1 Listen to 'All That Jazz' from *Chicago*. Analyse the piece by thinking about:

- the instruments it uses
- the context/venue it would be best performed in
- any other musical features you notice
- how it uses jazz chords.

Singing

2 As a class you are now going to sing 'All That Jazz'. Try to become familiar and confident with the song. It will help you with the rest of the tasks in this lesson.

3 Look at the notated version of the chord of C7 above. Discuss the effect of the extra note on the sound of the chord.

Performing

4 In pairs, learn to play the following riff from 'All That Jazz' on keyboards. The riff uses primary chords.
- Player 1 plays the C chord seven times followed by a rest.
- Player 2 plays the bass line riff based on the notes of C and G with an added note – A.
- You may be asked to perform your riff to the rest of the class.

Riff from 'All That Jazz'

5 Now prepare to perform the chord progression to 'All That Jazz'. It uses three types of chords:
- primary chords   • **added note chords**   • 7th chords (above).

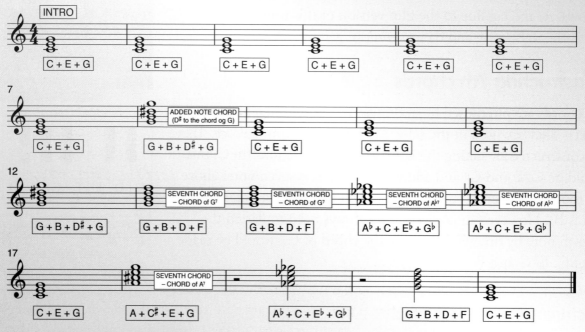

Chord progression from 'All That Jazz'

Appraising

6 As you listen to others in your class perform their chord progression, think about these questions.
  a Were the changes in chords smooth?
  b Could you sing the melody line of 'All That Jazz' along to the chord progression?
  c Was the performance well rehearsed?
  d How could the performance be improved?

Jazzing it up!

In this lesson you will:

- learn how chords can be used in your own jazz music

- learn to refine, rehearse, record, perform and evaluate your own and others' work.

Combining the features of jazz

Now that you have learnt about different chords and how these are used to create different effects, it is time for you to compose your own piece of jazz music using chords and the other features of jazz that you have read about.

Composing

1 Working in pairs or small groups, begin to plan your chordal jazz piece using the table below.
- Your piece should have four sections.
- The length of each section needs to be eight bars of four beats each.

SECTION 1 (eight bars):	SECTION 2 (eight bars):	SECTION 3 (eight bars):	SECTION 4 (eight bars):
Chord sequence using chords of C, F and G	Chord sequence using chords of C, F and G and improvisations	Chord sequence using 7th and added note chords	Chord sequence using chords of C, F and G and riffs

Section 1: composing your chord sequence
- Decide which chords you are going to use in which bar.
- Use only the chords of C, F and G and limit yourself to just one chord per bar.
- Start and end your eight-bar chord sequence on the same chord (C major).

Section 2: eight-bar improvisation
- Repeat your eight-bar chord sequence that you played in section 1.
- One of you will perform a melody improvisation using the notes of the blues scale (see page 9).
- Don't write your improvisation down, as it will be different every time you perform it.

Section 3: Composing a new eight-bar chord sequence

- Now use 7th chords and added note chords (look back at page 11 to remind yourself of these).
- Use two different 7th chords and two different added note chords.
- Remember, you can add any note to the basic chords of C, F and G.
- Adding different notes will create different effects, so experiment until you find a chord you like.
- Work out a chord sequence as you did in section 1 using your two added notes and two 7th chords. Combine some primary chords – for example C, F and G – if you like.

Section 4: Composing jazz riffs

- Use the chord sequence you composed in sections 1 and 2, but compose some jazz riffs as melodies to perform over the chords.
- Use notes from the chords to create your 'riffs' (remember how the melody of 'In the Mood' was taken from the notes of the chords – see lesson 1.2).

Now, you're ready to rehearse and perform your chordal jazz piece.

A jazz performance

From Transylvania to the Balkans

In this unit you will:

- learn about some of the main features of music from the Balkans
- learn what ornaments are and how they are used in music
- understand duple and triple metre and how they can be combined to produce heterometres
- recognise the fluid use of major and minor tonalities in music
- recognise the use of microtones in the music of other cultures

by:

- listening to traditional music from Serbia, Kosovo and Greece
- playing some Balkan style rhythms
- learning about the music of Bela Bartók
- performing a piece of kolo dance music individually and in groups
- performing a Croatian song as a whole class
- composing a piece of music in a Balkan style

because:

- it will introduce you to some new ideas and techniques which you can use in your own music
- playing heterometres will help you to develop your rhythmic skills
- ornaments are encountered in many different musical genres and eras
- using different scales and tunings can help to make your music more distinctive.

The rhythms of Hungary

In this lesson you will:

- learn about Bela Bartók's use of folk music in his compositions

- identify the use of heterometres in Balkan music.

The Balkans and Transylvania make up one of the most dynamic and fought-over parts of the world. The Balkan peninsula is a melting pot of different cultures where East meets West. It is here that Christianity meets the influence of Islam from Turkey and that the continents of Europe and Asia converge. Battles have been won and lost and maps redrawn by countless armies from the Romans to the Turks to the Austro-Hungarians. It is because of its unstable heritage that this area boasts some of Europe's richest and most vibrant music.

Bartók's use of Balkan folk music

As a young musician, the Hungarian composer Bela Bartók (1881–1945) overheard Lidi Dósa, a woman from Transylvania, singing the song *'Piros Alma'* ('Red Apple'). This chance event was the beginning of Bartók's lifelong fascination with folk music.
He studied the folk music of Hungary, Bulgaria, Croatia, Romania, Serbia and Turkey, and incorporated aspects of it into his own compositions.

Below is a **melody** from Bartók's collection of Hungarian peasant songs.

Bela Bartók

Listening to *'Ballade'*

5

1 Listen to a recording of *'Ballade'* by Bela Bartók, following the melody as you do so.
   a How many times is this melody played in total on the recording?
   b In what ways is the performance of the melody altered each time it is heard in order to keep the listener's attention? Try to identify at least three ways.
   c What would be an appropriate time signature for the music?

Focus on rhythm

In most western music, each bar is divided into regular groupings of beats. Rhythms in **duple metre** are divided into groups of two beats. Rhythms in **triple metre** are divided into groups of three beats. The first note in each group is emphasised in order to create a sense of pulse. Music from the Balkans often combines both duple and triple metre within the same bar. This technique creates rhythms that sound unconventional and unbalanced but exciting. These new rhythms are known as **heterometres** – 'hetero' meaning 'different' and 'metre' meaning 'grouping of beats'.

2 Look at the two rhythms below. Tap them on your knees using both right (R) and left (L) hands. Try to accent the first note in each group.

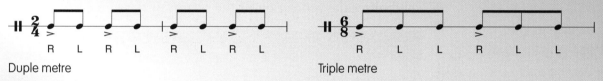

Duple metre   Triple metre

3 Now look at this new rhythm. Again, try tapping it on your knees and accenting the first note in each group.

Heterometre

4 The pattern in task 3 is a heterometre made up of 2 + 2 + 2 + 3 notes. Look back at Bartók's *Ballade* (task 1). What is the pattern of the heterometre there?

5 Now have a go at making up your own heterometre.
- Your heterometre should be between seven and thirteen quavers in length.
- It should contain a combination of duple and triple metre (groups of two and three quavers).
- Place accents at the start of each group of notes (add > underneath the accented notes).
- Show which hand you will use for which notes (usually you use one hand for the first note of each group and the other hand for the rest of them).
- Try playing your rhythm together as a group. If you can do this successfully on your knees, then you may be able to transfer it to instruments. If using a drum, use your hands in the manner you have indicated. Other instruments could just play the first (accented) note of each group.
- Prepare a performance for the rest of the class.

Serbian kolo

In this lesson you will:

- learn about the conventions of traditional kolo dance music

- learn to identify the expressive use of ornaments in music.

Ornaments

Ornaments are alterations to individual notes in a piece of music to add interest. They can be thought of as musical 'tricks' to keep the listener's interest alive. They include:

- trills *tr*⌇⌇⌇
  (two neighbouring notes played quickly, one after another)

- grace notes ♪
  (a note added before another as a decoration)

- glissandos *gliss.*
  (a technique where a musician slides from one note to another)

- mordents ⌁
  (a quick jump from the main note to the note above and then back again).

What is Kolo?

Serbia is in the heart of the Balkans. Away from the capital city, Belgrade, traditional music is still performed to mark important milestones in peoples' lives. Kolo is a popular Balkan dance in which the dancers hold hands, forming a circle. This tradition symbolises the protection of the community against evil.

Traditional Serbian Kolo dancing

Listening to *'Simfonijsko Kolo'*

7

1 You are about to hear a piece entitled *'Simfonijsko Kolo'*.
   As you listen, think about what makes this music ideal for dancing.

2 Follow the score (see page 19) as you listen again to *'Simfonijsko Kolo'*. This time, listen out for the **ornaments** in the music.

   a Can you hear these on the recording?

   b What does each sound like?

Performing

3 Now perform each ornament using your voice or an instrument.

   a Which is the shortest?

   b Which is the most difficult to play or sing?

4 The melody in *'Simfonijsko Kolo'* is made up of a number of eight-bar 'fragments', which are varied, contrasted and repeated. Rehearse this piece for a performance by following these steps.

- Make sure you can confidently clap the rhythm of your chosen part.
- Perform the melody on your instrument, focusing on correctly playing the pitches and rhythm.
- Check for ornaments and remind yourself how to play them. Add these when you are ready.
- Choose another part and repeat the process.
- If you are playing part 3, you can play either the upper note, the lower note or both.

Appraising

5 Your teacher may now invite you to perform one or more parts of *'Simfonijsko Kolo'*. Your performance will be appraised by others in the class. You will also be invited to appraise the work of others. Answer these questions to help you think about your own and others' performances.

   a Is there a steady beat to the music?

   b Are the pitches of the notes correct?

   c Are the ornaments included in the performance?

Tonality in Balkan music

In this lesson you will:

- learn about how major and minor scales are used in the Balkan music

- learn to arrange an ensemble performance of a piece of Serbian kolo.

Use of scales in Balkan music

When composing, many musicians choose a **tonality** or **key** for their piece. In other words, they stick to the notes and chords that belong to one particular scale – normally either a **major** or **minor** scale.

Music from Balkan countries is unusual because it sometimes uses **modulation** more frequently, changing from major to minor or vice versa. This means that the tonality appears to be more fluid than in some western music.

1 Below are the scales of C major and C minor. Which notes are shared by the two scales and which notes are different?

C major scale   C minor scale

Listening to *'Srpske igre I melodije sa Kosova'*

2 You are about to hear a Balkan melody called *'Srpske igre I melodije sa Kosova'.* This piece includes notes from both the major and minor version of the C scale. As you listen, follow the score below.
   a How do we know this pieces uses both C scales? The red notes are clues!
   b What effect does using notes from both scales have on the sound of the music?

'Srpske igre I melodije sa Kosova'

Performing

3 Return to your performance of *'Simfonijsko Kolo'* from lesson 2.2. *'Simfonijsko Kolo'* stays in the key of D major throughout. Work out and play the D major and minor scales.

4 Working in small groups, arrange an ensemble performance of the piece.

Towards the Mediterranean

In this lesson you will:

- learn about microtones and how they are used in Balkan music

- learn about the conventions of Croatian song, developing vocal techniques and musical expression.

Understanding microtones

From the 18th century onwards, it gradually became common in western music to divide the space between two notes an octave apart into twelve equal steps. This system, called **equal temperament**, is still used today and the twelve steps are known as **semitones**. These twelve steps make up the **chromatic scale**. For example, between two Cs you can find seven white keys and five black keys – the twelve **semitones**.

Not all musical cultures use this system. The space between two notes an octave apart may be divided into a greater or lesser number of steps or intervals. Ancient Greek music, for example, used scales which involved both larger and smaller intervals.

Intervals smaller than a semitone (known as **microtones**) are produced when an octave is divided into more than twelve steps. Microtones can be heard in the music of many cultures, such as those of Greece, India and Japan. The composer Charles Ives called microtones the 'notes between the cracks' of the piano.

Contemporary Greek musicians

Listening to 'Moustabeikos'

1 You are about to hear a piece of Greek music, 'Moustabeikos', which uses microtones. How does this music sound different to western music that uses the system of equal temperament?

Croatian song

Croatia is on the Adriatic coast of the Balkan peninsula. Croatian songs are often accompanied by a tanpura (a four-stringed instrument popular throughout Croatia) or are sung **a cappella** with voices harmonising each other.

A group of Croatian harmony singers

Listening to 'Lipa Moja'

🔘 10

2 Listen to the Croatian song *'Lipa Moja'*. As you do so, follow the lyrics below.

a What instruments can you hear?

b Singers often slide from one note to another, bending the pitch and in effect creating microtones. Think about jazz vocal music you have listened to. Can you think of any examples of where this happens? As you listen to *'Lipa Moja'* identify where the singers slide from one note to the next.

Lyrics for 'Lipa Moja'	*Phonetic transcription*
Lipa moja nacelo me vrime	*Leepah moyah nachelo may vreemay*
Kao mladu lozu u polju	*Cow mladoo lowzoo oo pol yoo*
A na skure zakucale zime, pa se tvoja mladost ruga	*Ana shkooray zakoo-chah-lay zeemay, pa say tvoya mladost roogahr*
Ovim neverama s juga ca nam prite	*Ovim neverama syoogah chanam preetay*
Lipa moja najlipsa od sviju	*Leepahr moyah nye-leepsa od sveeyoo*
Ponudi mi ljubav prid zoru	*Ponoodee mee yoobarv pree tzoroo*
I pusti da se divim tvome tilu, dok se tvoja mladost ruga	*Ee poostee da say deeveem tvomay teeloo, doksay tvoya mladost roogah*
Ovim neverama s juga ca nam prite	*Ovim neverama syoogah chanam preetay*
Lipa moja da te zvizde ne vide	*Leepahr mowyah datay zveesday nay veeday*
Ne bi znale s kim bi nebo dilile	*Ne bee znalay skeembee nebo deeleelay*
Lipa moja ti mi budi nevista	*Leepah mowyah teemee boodee nayveestah*
Budi krijesnica na mojim putima	*Boodee kryesneechah nar mowyeem pootimah*

Singing 'Lipa Moja'

3 You are about to sing *'Lipa Moja'* in a whole-class performance. Before you do so, focus on developing the following aspects, which are important for a good singing performance:

- clear diction
- good posture
- well-supported diaphragm
- co-ordinated points in the music where you can breathe
- confidence.

Balkan composition

In this lesson you will:

- learn to combine features of Balkan music in a composition.

Preparing your own piece

Throughout this unit you will have become familiar with the following features of music from the Balkans:

- increasing the tempo towards the end
- fluid major/minor tonality
- ornaments
- heterometres.

Another important musical feature that is sometimes used in the music of the Balkans is a drone.

Over the next two lessons, you will include some or all of these features in your own Balkan composition.

Composing dance music

1 In pairs or small groups, compose a short piece of dance music which includes the following elements:
  - a heterometre
  - a drone
  - a melody which moves between major and minor scales
  - ornaments
  - increasing the tempo (accelerando) towards the end.

Performing and appraising

2 Perform your compositions. Then assess your own and others' work by answering these questions for each group.
  - Which of the following parts could you hear?
    - melody   - rhythm   - drone.
  - Which of the following could you recognise in the composition?
    - an ornament   - heterometres   - simultaneous major and minor tonality.
  - Did each member of the group show awareness of, and sensitivity to, the others in the group?
  - What would you have improved in each group's composition or performance?

Improvisation and organisation

In this unit you will:

- learn about the contrast between improvised and organised sections of music
- explore how improvisation gives the performer the chance to 'show off' their technical ability
- explore how improvisation has commonly been used by a variety of composers in different times and places
- learn about the construction and workings of a pipe organ and traditional Indian musical instruments

by:

- listening to, performing and improvising a section from a Baroque organ toccata
- composing and performing an Indian raga to include an improvised section
- appraising different organ toccatas and Indian ragas, and making connections between the two genres
- listening to and appraising the use of the organ and traditional Indian musical instruments

because:

- improvisation and organisation are used in many different types of music
- exploring improvisation will help you to develop your own technical ability and flair
- looking at the similarities between organ toccatas and Indian ragas will help you to understand how music from different genres can share a common approach.

What is a toccata?

In this lesson you will:

- learn about Baroque organ toccatas and how they sound improvised

- explore how Baroque composers decorated their melodies.

The word **toccata** comes from the Italian word *'toccare'* meaning 'to touch'. It describes a piece of music, normally for a keyboard instrument, usually composed in a free style. Early toccatas used full chords and scale passages and were often played in a free tempo. Later, the toccata developed into a piece that was designed to show off the technical skills of the performer.

The features of a toccata

Toccatas have several different sections.

- Some sections sound organised and have a strict **pulse/meter**.
- Some sections sound **improvised** and have lots of fast running scale-like passages giving the performer a chance to display their keyboard talent.
- Some sections are played slowly with a **rubato** feel giving the performer freedom to play at their own speed.
- Composers such as Bach also used pauses in toccatas to create a feeling of tension and expectation, and melodies were decorated with extra notes (**mordents**).

Johann Sebastian Bach (1685–1750) was a German composer and organist from a well-established musical family. For much of his life, he held the position of organist in churches around Germany, and composed many works for the organ in addition to vocal and instrumental music.

Listening to 'Toccata in D minor'

1 a Listen to 'Toccata in D Minor' by J. S. Bach. Try to identify these musical features:
- starts and stops
- repetition
- melodic decoration
- musical pauses.

b What images or thoughts do you think of when listening to this piece of music?

c What differences can you hear between the sections of the music?

d What technical skills does the performer display?

e How does this piece of music give the organist a chance to 'show off' their technical skills?

Improvised or composed?

Although some sections of 'Toccata in D Minor' might sound improvised they are in fact all organised and even written down. Later in this unit, you will learn about the more aural tradition in Indian Classical music where performers improvise whole sections of music, following certain conventions.

Modern decorations

Famous contemporary singers like Mariah Carey and Celine Dion decorate vocal lines by adding improvisation sections, extra notes, singing very high pitched notes or singing notes of long duration to show off their vocal skill. Some guitarists also perform complicated solo passages in rock songs to show off their skills.

Performing lower mordents

Composers such as Bach often decorated their toccatas with complex musical devices such as **trills** and mordents to show off the player's skills. 'Toccata in D Minor' by J. S. Bach opens with a lower mordent. This has three notes:

   a the main note   (in Bach's example: A)

   b the note below   (in Bach's example: G)

   c the main note again   (in Bach's example: A)

The three notes of a lower mordent have to be performed as quickly as possible. The musical symbol for a lower mordent is ↯.

2 Try playing lower mordents on different notes on a keyboard until you can perform them quickly and smoothly.

3 How many ways can you think of to decorate a **melody** other than lower mordents?

Performing 'Toccata in D Minor'

4 Now that you can perform a lower mordent, practise performing the opening section of 'Toccata in D Minor'.

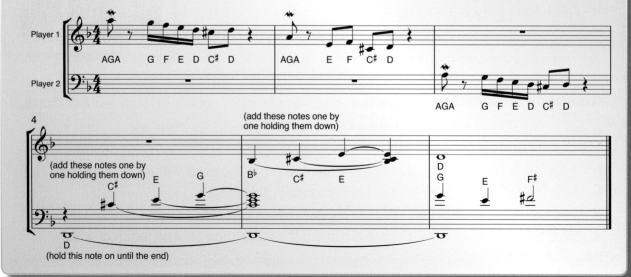

What makes a toccata?

In this lesson you will:

- learn how improvisation and organisation create musical contrast in a toccata

- use the D minor scale to perform improvised sections within a group performance of a toccata.

In lesson 3.1 you learnt about the toccata and some of its main features. You also started to perform the opening of Bach's 'Toccata in D minor'. Now you will have the opportunity to add some improvisation sections to your performance.

Improvising and performing

1 Using a tuned percussion instrument or a keyboard, improvise some passages using the scale of D minor shown below. Work in small groups, with one of you improvising while the others play a drone or pedal note on D.

D minor scale

2 Staying in your groups, add some improvised sections to your performance of 'Toccata in D minor'.
   a Begin your piece by playing the toccata theme that you began learning in lesson 3.1.
   b Next, one of you should perform an improvisation section using the notes of the D minor scale. The following guidelines may help you.
   - It is up to you to decide the length of each improvisation section – perhaps this will be different each time you perform your improvisation.
   - The people not improvising should play a drone or pedal note on D.
   - Think about some of the features used in toccatas – melodic decoration, pauses, contrasting fast and slow passages. Try to include some of these in your improvisation.
   - The person performing the improvisation should agree on a sign to indicate when they have finished.
   c When the improvisation section has finished, play the toccata theme as a group again.
   d Repeat this process, each time with a different member of the group performing the improvisation, until everyone has completed an improvised section.

Toccata in D minor with improvisations

In this lesson you will:

- refine, rehearse and perform 'Toccata in D minor with improvisations'
- learn about the features and workings of a pipe organ

- evaluate your own and others' work.

Performance time!

You are now ready to rehearse and perform your group piece 'Toccata in D minor with improvisations' to the rest of the class. Remember, your piece will be based on the following structure.

Toccata theme (whole group)	Improvisation 1 (solo) (other members to play pedal note D)	Toccata theme (whole group)	Improvisation 2 (solo) (other members to play pedal note D)	Toccata theme (whole group)	Improvisation 3 (solo) (other members to play pedal note D)	Toccata theme (whole group)

Performing and appraising

1 Perform your piece to the rest of the class, ensuring that each member of your group has the opportunity to improvise.

2 As you listen to other groups perform, identify any features they have used that Bach also used in his toccata.

3 Think about your group's performance.

  a Identify two good things about it.

  b Identify two things you would like to improve.

The pipe organ

The organ is capable of producing many different sounds. Some sound like orchestral instruments such as the flute, oboe and trumpet. Other sounds are unique to the organ. The pipe organ is powered by wind produced by a set of bellows. In the past, people would have to pump the bellows to make enough air to power the organ and to get it to sound, but today electric blowers are used to produce the wind.

When the organist pulls out a stop, they open a supply of wind to that set of pipes.

When they press a key on the manual, air is released into that pipe and a note sounds.

Organs have different manuals each with their own set of stops controlling different sets of pipes. The different stops on each manual are often at different pitches and timbres to give the organist a greater variety of sound.

The swell manual is situated at the very top of the organ. The organist can control the volume using the swell pedal.

There is sometimes a fourth manual called the solo or bombarde manual.

The pedals are played by the organist's feet. The pipes that belong to the pedals are clearly visible, as they are the largest in the organ. They are often placed in two large towers (called pedal towers) to the left and right of the organ.

Large organs have pistons between the manuals and above the pedals that the organist can use to set certain combinations of stops for sudden changes.

The choir manual contains soft, delicate stops to accompany the choir. It is found at the bottom of the console closest to the player, followed by the great and then the swell.

The great manual is the loudest manual and contains some of the most exciting stops on the organ.

What is a raga?

In this lesson you will:

- learn how Indian music is based on notes called a raga
- learn how different ragas have different moods
- learn how improvisations are based on the notes of a raga.

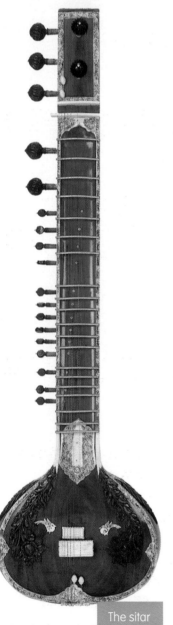

The sitar

The classical music of North India has been played in royal palaces and temples for more than 2000 years and is often closely associated with the Hindu religion. Indian classical music, like the Baroque organ toccata, is made up of different sections and textures. It uses improvisation to give the performer a chance to show off on their own instrument, and also to demonstrate their understanding of the music and its moods.

> **1** Why do you think western musicians and composers such as Bach wrote out their improvisation sections note by note, while Indian musicians leave this up to the performer? What different effects could this have on the music?

North Indian music

North Indian classical music is usually played by an ensemble of three people. This consists of:

- a main melody instrument (usually the sitar) or singer
- a percussion instrument – Indian drums called the tabla
- a drone instrument – the **tanpura** (a harmonium is also used).

Ragas

The melody of North Indian classical music is based on a pattern of notes called a **raga**. A raga is more like a melody than a scale. Each raga is intended for a particular time of day and has its own special mood such as happiness, courage, humour, peace, sadness or anger. Ragas are often left completely up to the performer – that is, musicians do not play from fixed notation worked out beforehand by a composer (such as Bach).

Raga moods

According to the mood, each raga belongs to a particular season (for example, for planting crops or monsoon rains) or a different time of day (there are morning, afternoon, evening and night ragas). Indian musicians do not announce the raga they are going to play until the time of the concert depending on their own personal mood.

2 Music is based on many different types of scales and modes. How many can you name? Can you remember how to construct or perform any of these scales and modes?

Performing

3 Below are three different ragas, each belonging to a different part of the day and mood.

Morning raga ('*Vibhas*')
Mood: sound of the early dawn

Drone notes C, A

Evening raga ('*Behag*')
Mood: peaceful and relaxed

Drone notes C, G

Night raga ('*Malakosh*')
Mood: peaceful and relaxed

Drone notes B, E

a Work in pairs and play through each of the ragas using the guidelines below.
  • Choose a suitable instrument (such as a glockenspiel or xylophone, or an appropriate timbre on a keyboard – you may even find a sitar timbre!) and play through each of the three ragas.
  • One person should perform using the notes of the raga while the other performs the drone notes.
  • Take your time and experiment with the various shapes the melody makes. Notice the mood of each raga – try and use this 'feeling' in your improvisations, as this is very important in Indian music.
b Listen carefully to each raga. How is the first one different to the second and third?
c Now choose one of the ragas above and use it as a basis for an improvisation to perform to the rest of the class. Remember: you are improvising so when you perform it will be different each time!

Dha Dhin Dhin Dha

In this lesson you will:

- improvise within a tala rhythm
- compose your own gat section.

The tala is played on Indian tabla drums

The tala

The beat or rhythm that accompanies an Indian raga is called the tala. It is a repeated rhythmic pattern – for example 10, 12 or 16 beats – that is arranged in a repeating cycle. In this lesson you will focus on improvising rhythms to the tala and composing a gat secion for your raga.

Improvising on tala

1 Working in pairs, perform a traditional Indian tala. One of you should perform the tala while the other improvises rhythms patterns to fit with it. The cycle is shown below (X = very stong beat; O = very weak beat.).

```
X                    -                    O                    -
1   2   3   4 ┊ 5   6   7   8 ┊ 9   10  11  12 ┊13  14  15  16
Dha dhin dhin dha   Dha dhin dhin dha   Dha tin  tin  ta   Ta   dhin dhin da
```

- Perform the tala with the different actions on beats 1, 5, 9 and 13.
- You could mark the intervening beats by placing your thumb on three fingers in turn (middle, index and ring).
- When you are both confident playing the tala, one of you should improvise rhythms on the drums in time with the beat.
- Take turns so that both of you have a chance to improvise rhythms.

Composing your own gat section

2 Working in groups of four, compose another section of your raga called the gat. This combines four elements: a drone, improvisation using the raga scale, the tala, and rhythmic improvisation. Choose one of the ragas that you worked on in the previous lesson. Decide who will play which part:
- Player A: drone
- Player B: improvise using notes of the raga scale
- Player C: tala
- Player D: rhythmic improvisation.
You may be asked to perform your gat to the rest of the class at the end of the lesson.

East meets West

In this lesson you will:

- refine, rehearse, perform and evaluate your own and others' work

- learn how improvisation has been used as a feature in music from different times and different places.

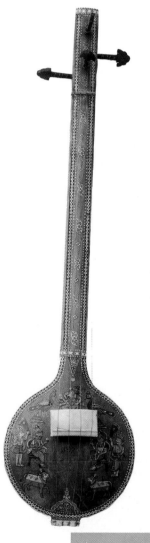

The tanpura

The structure of an Indian raga

The structure of an Indian raga is made up of four different sections. You composed and performed the first section of a raga – the **alap** – in lesson 3.4 and the third section – the gat – in lesson 3.5. Look at the four sections of a raga in the table below.

Section	Description
Alap	This is the first section of a raga. In this section, the melody instrument (sitar), introduces and explores the notes of the chosen raga. The mood of the alap section is peaceful with no sense of rhythm and is accompanied by the drone (tambura).
Jor	This section is where the melody instrument (sitar) and drone (tanpura) continue to play but slowly increase in tempo and play to a more steady pulse.
Gat	This section is where the drums (tabla) are introduced and begin playing the tala rhythm cycles. The tabla player improvises on the tala while the solo melody instruments (sitar) improvises on the notes of the raga.
Jhalla	This is the last section of a raga. Here all three instruments increase in tempo playing faster and faster until they reach a rhythmic climax.

Rehearsing and performing an Indian raga

1 In this lesson you will be give time to refine, rehearse and perform your raga composition. This will have four sections:
  - alap – you can use the ideas you worked on in lesson 3.4
  - jor – something to link your alap with your gat
  - gat – which you worked on in lesson 3.5
  - jhalla – a lively ending.

  First, rehearse the two sections you have already worked on. Then you can decide how to link the two sections, and how to finish your piece. You will then be asked to perform it to the rest of the class.

2 As you listen to the performances of other groups, think about the how the piece has been built up. Listen out for the melodic raga, the drone, the tala, melodic improvisation on the raga and rhythmic improvisation on the tala.
  a What made the difference between a successful piece and a not-so successful piece?
  b What were the most successful features of your piece?
  c Which of the groups was the most successful and why?

East meets West: improvisation and organisation

The Baroque organ toccata and Indian raga both contain elements of improvisation and organisation. How are they similar and how are they different?

Listening

11 & 16

3 Listen to two different pieces of music: an organ toccata and a traditional Indian raga.
  a Compare the two pieces of music noting down any similarities and differences. In particular, listen out for texture and structure.
  b Which of the two pieces of music do you prefer? Why?
  c Why do you think that musicians use improvisation when performing music?
  d What other types and styles of music use improvisation?

An Indian raga performance

Polyrhythm into minimalism

In this unit you will:

- learn how cyclic rhythms and polyrhythms are used in traditional African drumming music
- explore how to use rhythm grids and rhythm notation when composing and performing
- find out about the key musical features of minimalist music and how it is constructed
- learn how to combine and manipulate different motifs when performing and composing a piece of minimalist music

by:

- performing a repeated rhythm as a cyclic rhythm pattern
- layering rhythms over the top of each other to form a polyrhythmic texture
- notating rhythms using rhythm grids
- listening to and performing two minimalist pieces, 'Clapping Music' and 'Tubular Bells', which use rhythmic and melodic motifs
- composing your own minimalist piece of music, carefully selecting and combining motifs to produce an intended effect and style

because:

- being able to maintain your own rhythm as part of a group texture increases your skill and confidence in performing
- writing your music down is an important way of keeping track of your ideas
- minimalism is a style of music that uses and combines features from different genres of music
- composing a minimalist piece using simple musical ingredients will help you to develop your composition skills.

African drumming

In this lesson you will:

- learn about the different techniques used in African drumming to create different tones and sounds

- explore the features of rhythms used in African drumming.

Learning about the music of Africa

A selection of African drums; the most common form of African drum is called the **djembe**

The people of Africa use many different instruments to make their music, but the most popular are drums. African drums come in every shape and size. Some have various kinds of skins, whereas others may have long slits in the trunk instead. Drums can have one, two, three or more tones. They are played with large or small sticks, hands or both. Some drums are put together in a cluster, each having a different pitch. There are even drums whose pitch can be modified while being played!

Rhythm in African music

Rhythm is the core of all African drumming music. Some rhythms, called **cyclic** rhythms, are repeated over and over again. Sometimes a duo or a group of drummers play different rhythms at the same time, starting and stopping at different times to create a thick texture – this is called **polyrhythm**.

Performing: how to play an African drum

1 Most African drums are played by hand. Sticks are occasionally used depending on the type of drum. Try playing the drum following the instructions below.
- Relax your hands and fingers.
- Hold your fingers close together and strike the top of the drum.
- Do not hit the drum too hard: doing so will hurt your hands and could damage the drum.
- Once you have hit the drum, let your hands bounce off the top of the drum head and allow it to resonate. If you do not bounce your hand off the drum it will not resonate and instead will produce a 'dead' sound.

2 There are two main sounds used in African drumming.
- The bass sound: this is achieved by striking the drum in the middle (especially if it is a djembe).
- The tone sound: this is achieved by striking the drum between the centre and the edge.

The third sound that can be produced is the slap sound. This takes a lot of practice and there are two ways of making it.
- Cup your hand slightly, then strike the drum with your fingers.
- Rest your weaker hand in the middle of the drum, then strike the side or open sound position of the drum with your other hand.

Try producing each of these different sounds on a drum.

Performing: 'Sun Over the Sahara'

3 You now have chance to perform the duns (bass line) to an African-style piece of music called 'Sun Over the Sahara'. The bass parts provide the main rhythmical structure for the whole piece. They are like a musical foundation.

a Focus first getting the rhythms correct and on hitting the drum in the right place and in the right way to make the correct sound.

b In groups, divide into two halves: one should perform Part A, while the other performs Part B. Use the following key for the different hits on the drum:

B = bass sound

T = tone sound

Part A

1	+	2	+	3	+	4	+
B		B		T T			

Part B

1	+	2	+	3	+	4	+
	B	T T	B			T	T

Rhythms of Africa

In this lesson you will:

- use rhythm notation to record your ideas
- compose and perform a group polyrhythmic piece.

Polyrhythm

As you learnt in the previous lesson, rhythm is a central element of African music. A polyrhythmic texture can be achieved by playing different rhythms at the same time.

Performing a polyrhythmic piece

1 You are about to perform a piece based on African rhythms. Each of the rhythms will be repeated over and over to form a cyclic rhythm. These cyclic rhythms will then be added to another group's rhythm until all the groups in the class are performing their own cyclic rhythms to form a polyrhythmic texture.

a As a class perform each of the rhythms from the grid below.

b Divide into four groups and move into a different area of the classroom with your group. Each group should take one of the rhythms below and repeat it over and over, turning it into a cyclic rhythm.

c With each group still performing their different rhythms, gradually move closer and closer to the centre of the class, getting louder and louder and creating a polyrhythmic texture. When the groups meet, gradually move apart again so the dynamics become quieter.

●		●	●			●		●	●		
●		●		●		●		●		●	
●			●		●		●			●	
●		●		●	●		●		●	●	

Composing

2 Working in groups of four, compose your own polyrhythm piece using the guidelines below.

- Each member of the group will need to decide on their own rhythm.
- You may find it helpful to notate the rhythms of your piece using a rhythm grid like the example below.

	1	2	3	4	5	6	7	8	9	10	11	12
Part A												
Part B												
Part C												
Part D												

- As a group, decide on an appropriate structure for your composition. To start with only one player should perform their rhythm. It is up to the group to decide on appropriate points for other rhythms to be added until all members of the group are performing together in a polyrhythmic texture.
- Think of an appropriate way to end your piece.

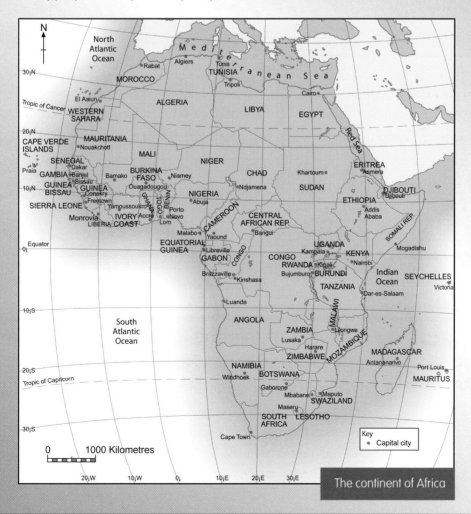

The continent of Africa

'Clapping Music' – but is it music?

In this lesson you will:

- learn about the development and conventions of minimalism
- explore how minimalist composers use short rhythmic motifs to build a bigger piece.

Minimalism

Like impressionism, minimalism was originally a style in art before it became a type of music. Minimalist art is a type of art in which objects are stripped down to their basic geometric form and presented in an impersonal manner. It is an **abstract** style of art. When the term 'minimal' is used in music, it means compositions that are created with the most basic and limited amount of material.

How do you feel about this piece of art? Is this really art at all?

Erik Satie

The composer Erik Satie (1866–1925) composed a piece of music called 'Vexations', which is perhaps the first example of minimalist music. It consists of a short phrase repeated 840 times without variation!

Features of minimalist music

Minimalist music draws on a number of features from different types and styles of music, including those from African music such as repetition, cyclic rhythms and polyrhythms. The main feature of minimalist music is a limited number of short, melodic, rhythmic and harmonic patterns (called **motifs**) that are repeated again and again. These patterns often give the music a hypnotic effect.

'The Monotonous School'

As minimalist music is quite repetitive, a group of four American minimalist composers (Steve Reich, La Monte Young, Philip Glass, and Terry Riley) were given the nickname 'The Monotonous School'. However, many of their works are full of rhythmic excitement, rich timbres and harmonic colours. This tends to result from a layering of different motifs and ostinati, which merge to create complex structures of rhythm and pitch.

Traditional western European music uses ostinati and repetition, but the four American composers have also been influenced by Indian, Balinese Gamelan and West African music, especially in the use of uneven or irregular rhythmic patterns.

The minimalist composers Steve Reich and Philip Glass

Listening to 'Clapping Music'

18

Steve Reich composed 'Clapping Music for Two Performers' in 1972. Reich wanted to perform a piece needing only the human body and decided to use the sound of a human clap as a basis for his piece. 'Clapping Music' uses just one rhythmic motif. One person plays this motif all the time while the other displaces this motif by one beat and repeats this new pattern 12 times.

1 Listen to 'Clapping Music' and answer the following questions.
   a What happens to the pulse in the music? Does it speed up, slow down or stay the same?
   b Can you tell when one of the performers changes their rhythmic motif and begins to clap a new one? What effect does this have on the music?
   c What do you think of this piece of music? Is this really music at all?

Composing your own 'Clapping Music'

2 Working in groups create your own piece of 'Clapping Music'. Try to make use of the musical devices that Steve Reich used in his composition.
   • Begin by creating a motif and writing it in a grid.
   • Once you have your motif, create a pattern by displacing your motif by one beat each time – forwards or backwards … it's up to you!
   • Divide into two groups. One group plays the motif while the others work through the other lines, clapping each one an agreed number of times.
   • Experiment with some different ideas for combining the rhythms and prepare your piece for performance.

'Tubular Bells'

In this lesson you will:

- learn how melodic motifs can be used to create a piece of minimalist music
- explore the effect of combining and manipulating different melodic motifs.

Mike Oldfield and 'Tubular Bells'

Minimalism often makes use of repeating patterns of music (motifs) that subtly change. This gradual change means that the 'feel' of the music stays the same but the listener does not get bored. This is how Mike Oldfield composed his famous piece 'Tubular Bells' in 1972.

Composer Mike Oldfield

Mike Oldfield began by recording a 20-minute demo tape of multi-tracked guitar parts onto a cheap tape machine and submitted this to Virgin Records. He was given a record deal and set about recording 'Tubular Bells', playing almost every part of the music himself. He gradually layered sound upon sound, following the style of a minimalist composer, and mixed unusual instrument tones together such as the flageolet, glockenspiel and, of course, tubular bells.

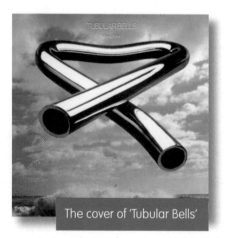

The cover of 'Tubular Bells'

Listening to 'Tubular Bells' 19

1 As you listen to the opening of 'Tubular Bells', notice how the piece starts off with a simple melodic motif, and how each new motif is then brought in gradually (**phased in**) so that the texture of the music becomes denser as more sounds are added.

Performing 'Tubular Bells'

2 You will now have the opportunity to play 'Tubular Bells' yourself. Follow the step-by-step instructions below.

- Practise playing each of the four motifs from 'Tubular Bells' as shown below.
- In groups of four, choose appropriate instruments and sounds for each part. Put the four layers together (the **melody** and harmony parts need to repeat four times for *each* repeat of the chords and bass line).
- Make your own arrangement of the piece by deciding when each part should start (phase in).
- Once all the parts are playing together, try making small, gradual changes to each part as the piece progresses. Think carefully about what you will change (for example the texture, the timbre of your instruments, the dynamics and so on).
- Do not feel that you have to play your part all the time – parts dropping out for a while can have as big an impact as parts joining in, and this is a key feature of minimalist music.

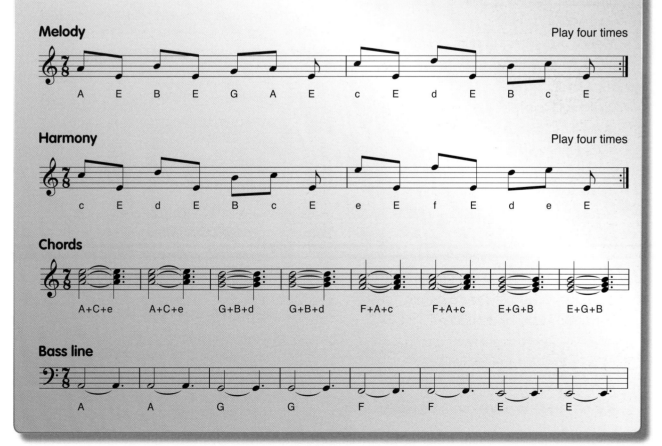

Composing your own minimalist piece

In this lesson you will:

- learn how to select and combine melodic motifs to create a minimalist piece of music.

Composing

Now that you have learnt about how minimalist composers have used only the most basic and limited amount of material, you are going to compose your own minimalist-style piece of music in groups. Due to the 'free' nature of minimalist music, much of the composition will be up to you, such as the instruments and timbres used. Follow the guidelines below when putting together your composition.

- Choose an object or a theme as inspiration for your minimalist piece and give your piece a title.
- Each member of the group will need to create their own motif. This can be based on as few notes as you think appropriate for your composition.
- Decide which instruments your group will use and what timbres you will use.
- Make a plan of the structure of your piece. Who will begin and who will come in phase next?
- Remember: a key feature of minimalism is each new motif being added gradually, so that there are subtle changes on the listener.
- Allow some parts to go out of phase so that not all of the motifs are played together.
- Finally, compose an ending for your piece. You might like to compose a dramatic ending with the dynamics becoming louder and louder. Alternatively, you might want your piece to fade out and become quieter.

This piece of minimalist art, called 'Hyena Stomp' is based on a song by the same name. The artist, Frank Stella, was thinking about syncopation while working on this painting.

Music for special occasions

In this unit you will:

- learn how music is associated with different special occasions, events and ceremonies
- explore how composers combine the elements of music in order to create music suitable for different special occasions
- learn about the demands upon composers who are commissioned to write music for a special occasion

by:

- listening to and identifying features in music suitable for a range of special occasions, events and ceremonies
- performing a range of music written for special occasions
- composing your own music for special occasions in response to a commission

because:

- music plays an important part in many special occasions, events and ceremonies
- learning about the way in which composers use the elements of music will help you in your own compositions
- learning about how composers are commissioned to write music will help you consider factors in your own music.

Music for an occasion

In this lesson you will:

- learn how music is associated with different special occasions, events and ceremonies
- learn about fanfares

- learn to recognise musical features in different pieces of music for special occasions.

Music and events

Sometimes, composers are asked to write music for a special occasion – for example, a coronation, or a sporting event. The only real rules are that the music must be appropriate for the occasion.

Listening to music for a special occasion

 21, 22 & 23

1 Listen to three pieces of music, each of which is connected with a special occasion, location, event or ceremony. As you listen to the music, match it to a–c below.

  a An opera house   **b** A cathedral service

  c Folk dancing (Morris Men)

2 Describe why you made your choices for matching the music. Which features in the music led you to make these choices? Try to use musical terms to explain your answers.

Fanfares

Military guards playing bugles as part of a fanfare

A **fanfare** is 'a loud short piece of music, played, usually on a trumpet, to introduce the arrival of someone important or a special event'. Since medieval times, fanfares have been used to herald the entrance of a king, queen or other important person. Fanfares have also been used for many years on military occasions and on the battlefield as a signal that troops can hear and act on.

The harmonic series

Modern-day trumpets have three valves, which the player uses to open or close different lengths of tubing to produce notes of many different **pitches**. In earlier times, trumpets, like **bugles**, had no valves and could only play a limited range of notes. These notes were called the **harmonic series** and most early fanfares use only these notes. The most relevant notes used in bugle calls and fanfares are taken from the harmonic series.

C   G   C   E   G   C

Notes from the harmonic series

A valveless trumpet

Listening and performing

 24

3 Listen to part of Mendelssohn's 'Wedding March'. The piece begins with a short fanfare. What effect does this create?

4 Working in groups of two or three, perform the opening fanfare following the score below.

Opening fanfare from Mendelssohn's 'Wedding March'

Composing

5 Working in pairs or small groups, start to develop your own ideas for a fanfare using two additional features that your teacher will demonstrate to you: **passing notes** and **imitation**. You will build on these ideas in the next lesson.

Fanfares!

In this lesson you will:

- learn about the key features of a fanfare
- learn about the demands on composers who are commissioned to write music for a special occasion
- learn how to compose your own fanfare for a special occasion.

Aaron Copland

'Fanfare for the Common Man'

One of the best known modern fanfares is 'Fanfare for the Common Man', written by the American composer Aaron Copland.

In the middle of World War II, an English conductor called Eugene Goosens asked Copland to compose a fanfare for the Cincinnati Symphony Orchestra. Copland's fanfare was an immediate success when it was premiered on 12 March 1943 and has remained one of the most famous fanfares ever since. In his autobiography, the composer says: 'The challenge was to compose a traditional fanfare, direct and powerful, yet with a contemporary sound.'

Listening to 'Fanfare for the Common Man'

 25

1 Listen to 'Fanfare for the Common Man'. As you do so, jot down the answers to these questions.
  a The fanfare starts with an introduction before the **melody** begins. What instruments are playing in the introduction? Which family of the orchestra do they come from?
  b What is the first **brass** instrument you hear that plays the melody?
  c Do the pitches of the opening three notes of the melody get higher or lower?
  d What other brass instruments do we hear playing in the fanfare?
  e What happens to the dynamics in the fanfare?
  f What about the texture?
  g At what sort of special occasions or events do you think it would be suitable to play 'Fanfare for the Common Man'? Why?

Composing a fanfare

2 Imagine you have received a **commission** from your head teacher to compose a fanfare for a special occasion at school – for example, a sports day or award ceremony. In groups, think about how you will meet this commission.

- What sort of things do you need to think about before you start writing your fanfare? Think about what you learnt about fanfares from lesson 5.1. Which of these might you be able to use in your composition?
- How will you combine the elements of music to reinforce the atmosphere and **mood** of the event?
- Remember to record your ideas using staff or graphic notation.

You will be assessed later on whether your composition successfully includes the following criteria.

a Use the notes of the harmonic series for your fanfare melody.

C   G   C   E   G   C

b Add any other features you think you want to use:
- passing notes
- echo effect
- dynamics
- percussion instruments.

c Think about the structure of your piece. How will it begin and end?

d Finally, think carefully about whether your piece is suitable for your chosen special occasion. Can it be improved in any way?

Performing and assessment

3 Perform your fanfare to the rest of the class. Your performance may be recorded. Others in your class will be invited to assess your piece using criteria a–d above.

4 Now using the criteria above assess your own work. Also think about:
- **two** features you liked about your group's fanfare
- **two** things you would do differently if you were to compose a fanfare again.

Music for funerals

In this lesson you will:

- learn how a Baroque composer was commissioned to write music for the funeral of Queen Mary

- learn about the features used in funeral music to create a sad mood suited to the occasion.

Listening

 27 & 28

1 You are about to hear two excerpts of music.
  a What sort of special occasion would this music be played at?
  b What are the similarities and differences of these excerpts?

Henry Purcell

'Funeral Music for Queen Mary'

When Queen Mary died of smallpox in 1694, the English composer Henry Purcell was commissioned to write some suitable music to be played at her funeral in Westminster Abbey, London. Purcell was 'Master of the King's Musick' and was responsible for all music connected with the royal family.

Purcell had to think carefully about his commission and came up with music in a **minor** key to represent the sadness and solemn occasion he was writing for. He used brass instruments, similar to those used in fanfares, to show the importance of the Queen.

Part of the music, entitled 'March', has instructions that Purcell himself wrote – to be 'sounded before her chariot' (the horse-drawn hearse). The piece has a **homophonic texture** where the brass instruments play together in a block chordal texture.

The part entitled 'Canzona' was played during the Queen's burial. This piece has a different texture with each brass instrument having an individual line that plays against the other parts together.

Performing

2 In pairs, you are about to perform part of 'Funeral March'. The score is given below. One of you should play the melody; the other should play the minor chords. This piece uses two minor chords – the chord of D minor and the chord of G minor. Think about the instrument sound you will use on your keyboard, the tempo and choose a timbre suited to the mood of the occasion.

The chord of D minor is made up of three notes – D, F, A

The chord of G minor is made up of three notes – G, B♭, D

'Funeral March'

Composing

3 When you are confident playing the 'Funeral March', compose an additional section. Here are some ideas to help you.

- Use the scale of D minor to keep a sad feel to the music.

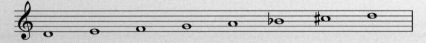

- Use the chords of D and G minor.
- Add an ostinato or a drone to your new section.

Finally, perform the 'Funeral March' and your additional section in **ternary** form – A B A.

Music for weddings

In this lesson you will:

- learn how composers have used musical elements and devices in pieces of music used at weddings

- understand how different parts fit together to form a piece of wedding music.

Bridal and wedding marches

A bridal or wedding march is a piece of music played during a wedding, usually during the entrance of the bride. A similar piece of music is used to mark the end of the ceremony where the married couple depart. The tempo needs to be 'stately' rather than fast, as the bride and groom have to walk (not dance!) to the music.

Listening to wedding music

 24, 29 & 30

1 You are about to listen to three pieces of music that are frequently played at weddings.

a As you listen, pick out the features you can hear in each piece of music. (Some features may be used in all the pieces and some not at all.)

- Begins with a short fanfare
- Question and answer (call and response) phrases
- Minor key
- Played by an organ
- Played by an orchestra
- Ternary form (A B A)

- **March**
- Pedal notes
- Contrasting sections
- Stately and grand mood
- Sad and sombre mood
- Slow tempo
- Fast tempo
- Loud dynamics

- Drums
- **Trills**
- Binary form (A B)
- Fanfare returns in the middle of piece
- Major key
- **Ostinato**

b Were you uncertain about any of the features?

c What conclusions can you make about music suitable for weddings?

Famous wedding marches

The 'Bridal March' from Wagner's opera *Lohengrin* is probably the most famous piece of wedding music of all time. It is most commonly heard at traditional Christian weddings in the West as the bride enters the church. The features common to this type of music (for example, a slow stately tempo) that you identified for task 1 make the music suitable for this purpose.

Another famous piece is the 'Wedding March' by Mendelssohn, the opening of which you learnt to play in lesson 5.1. This piece is often played at the end of the ceremony.

Both of these pieces open with a short fanfare. The music is in a major key to signify the happiness of the special occasion and is played at a moderate tempo so that the bride can literally 'march' up the aisle.

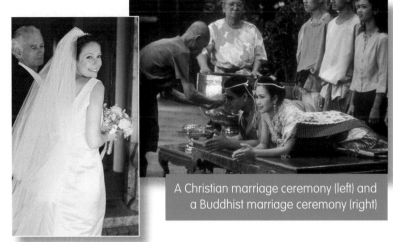

A Christian marriage ceremony (left) and a Buddhist marriage ceremony (right)

Performing 'Bridal March'

2 You are about to learn one of the parts to the 'Bridal March' as part of a class performance.
- Part 1 is the famous melody as composed by Wagner.
- Part 2 is the bass line.

Decide which part you will play. Your teacher will help with this. If you are playing an instrument that you are learning, that may dictate which part you will perform.

Part 1: Melody to the Bridal March

Part 2: Bass to the Bridal March

Composing your own special occasion music

In this lesson you will:

- use your knowledge of music for special occasions to compose your own piece for a special occasion of your choice

- rehearse and refine your special occasion composition and perform it to the rest of the class.

Your own composition

To end this unit of work, you will compose and perform a piece of music that will be played at a special occasion. The choice of special occasion is up to you, but your music needs to reflect very carefully the type or style of the occasion, the audience and the venue.

Composing and performing

You are about to compose and perform a piece of special occasion music for the rest of the class. Don't give any clues about the occasion. See if the rest of the class can identify it after your performance. Think about the following when composing your music.

1 Think about the event you have chosen. How will that influence the feel of the music?
- What types of sound will you use?
- What instruments will you use?

2 Now think about tempo: should your piece be fast or slow? Should it get faster or slower? Should it feel like a march?

Special occasion:
_____

3 What sort of dynamics will your piece have? Will it be loud or quiet? Will the dynamics change.

4 Think of a tune for your piece. What should it be describing? How will it help to create the right 'feel' for your piece?

5 Add an accompaniment. You could use:
- chords
- an ostinato
- percussion rhythms
- a drone.

6 Now you need to rehearse, perform and evaluate your composition.

Making arrangements

In this unit you will:

- learn how composers have used musical elements and devices to create variations on different themes
- learn how to make your own variations to a theme
- learn about the different components that make up a performance of a song
- learn how to make different arrangements of popular songs from different times and places

by:

- listening to pieces in variation form and identifying the techniques used
- composing a set of four different musical variations on a theme
- taking part in a class performance of a popular song
- making your own arrangement of a popular song

because:

- it will give you ideas for exploring themes in different ways
- it will show you how you can make arrangements of songs to suit your own abilities and tastes
- it will help you to recap you learning about musical devices and techniques from across the Key Stage.

Variations

In this lesson you will:

- learn how a theme can be arranged in different ways using variation form

- use variation techniques in your own musical arrangements.

Charles Edward Ives

(1874–1954) was an American composer. He is widely regarded as one of the first American classical composers of international significance. His work as an organist led him to compose *Variations on 'America'* in 1891, which he premiered at a recital celebrating the Fourth of July. The piece takes the theme through a series of musical arrangements called 'variations'. Another composer, William Schuman, arranged Ives' variations for orchestra in 1964.

Variations as a form of musical arrangement

Many composers have taken a **theme** and used it in different ways to create a different musical **arrangement**. Manipulating the elements of music such as pitch, tempo, dynamics, duration, texture and timbre gives a theme a different effect. Other composers have used musical devices such as a **drone**, **ostinato**, **counter-melody** or a **round**. Mozart used the tune of a French song which we know as 'Twinkle, Twinkle, Little Star', then wrote a series of **variations** on it, each using musical devices and features that created a different musical effect and mood.

Variation is one way to create a musical arrangement. An arrangement is when you select, manipulate and change different aspects of the music or theme to create something that is based on an original idea but with your own personal features. Many popular songs are arrangements (or cover versions) of older songs.

Listening to variations

1 You are going to listen to Ives' theme and five variations on the original theme. Notice how these variations have their own individual style and character. For each one, note down the features and elements you can hear. Use as many musical words in your answers as you can. You might like to think about:

- the number of beats in a bar
- major/minor key
- dynamics
- tempo
- use of chords
- accompaniment
- ostinato
- rhythm
- counter melody
- Spanish dance-style arrangement
- instruments used.

You might also like to think about how each variation differs from the original theme.

Composing variations

2 Work in pairs and compose your own set of variations on 'God Save the Queen' or on a theme of your choice. You might even like to write your own theme as a basis for your variations.

- First, learn to play whatever theme you choose until you can perform it really well.
- Next, think about how you will create different variations on your theme (as Ives did for 'America'). Remember, each variation should have its own mood and character.
- Think about how you can change the elements of music and other musical devices to create variations that are different, yet still based on the original theme.
- Use what you learnt from task 1 to help you with your variations.
- You can compose as many variations as you like.
- You will continue work on your variations in lesson 6.2.

Theme of 'God Save the Queen' in F major

A theme, but not as we know it!

In this lesson you will:

- construct a set of musical variations on a given theme
- evaluate the effectiveness of variation techniques used.

More on variations

In lesson 6.1, you learnt about the composer Charles Ives. Another American composer who used variations on a theme was Aaron Copland (1900–90). You may recall that you listened to one of his compositions, 'Fanfare for the Common Man', in Unit 5 (Music for special occasions).

Copland incorporated into his compositions popular forms of American music such as jazz and folk to create exciting and inspiring pieces. In 1944 he wrote *Appalachian Spring* for the famous dancer Martha Graham. The music describes the gentler side of the American Wild West. In one of the movements, 'Variations on a Shaker Tune', Copland uses a tune known in America as 'Simple Gifts'. He composed a set of variations designed to show scenes of daily life and work for a bride and her farmer husband.

A scene from the ballet *Appalachian Spring* by Aaron Copland

Listening to 'Variations on a Shaker Tune'   **37**

1 You are about to listen to 'Variations on a Shaker Tune' from Copland's *Appalachian Spring*. As you do so, follow the listening map and answer the questions.

TIMING IN MUSIC	THEME/VARIATION	QUESTIONS
00:00–00:30 secs	Theme	• What instrument is playing the theme? • What instruments accompany the theme?
0:31–0:50 secs	Variation 1	Two instruments play the theme in this variation like a musical conversation. • What is the name for this? • Which two instruments are playing the theme? • How would you describe the texture?
0:51–1:28 secs/mins	Variation 2	• What has happened to the pitch of the theme? • The theme is played in an 'overlapping' style by the strings. What is the musical name for this?
1:29–1:57 mins	Variation 3	• Which family of instruments plays the theme in this variation? • What has happened to the tempo and dynamics of the theme in this variation?
1:58–2:11 mins	Variation 4	• Which family of instruments plays the theme? • How do the dynamics of this variation compare with Variation 3?
2:12–2:43 mins	Variation 5	• How would you describe the dynamics and texture? • What percussion instruments can you hear? • How would you describe its mood?

Performing and composing

2 Now that you have heard how another composer has used variations to change and modify a theme, see if there are any new ideas that you can use in the variations you began in lesson 6.1.

3 Rehearse your variations. You will be asked to perform your pieces to the rest of the class. Your piece will also be recorded and evaluated by both you and your classmates.
  • Remember that each of your variations should have a different mood.
  • Remember to record all of your ideas for each variation.

'Stand By Me'

In this lesson you will:

- learn how songs can be performed in different styles to create different effects
- learn how instrumentation, textural layers and structure can create an effective arrangement of a popular song
- create an arrangement of a popular song in a different style
- assess and evaluate your own and other's musical arrangements.

Ben E. King

Background to 'Stand By Me'

'Stand by Me' was co-written and recorded by Ben E. King shortly after he left a pop group called The Drifters in 1960. The song, which started as a gospel-style piece, gave him a solid reputation as a solo artist. 'Stand By Me' was given a more contemporary arrangement, plus its famous bass line, by two successful songwriters of the 1960s, Jerry Leiber and Mike Stoller.

Listening to 'Stand By Me'

38 & 39

1 You are about to hear and compare two versions of the song 'Stand By Me'. One is the original and the other is an arrangement. For the arrangement, the musicians have tried to:

- adapt the song to meet their own instrumental and vocal resources in performance
- update the song with new material that reflects their own personal style.

As you listen, think about the features below that describe what is happening. Make a note of which features appear in which song (some may be heard in more than one version, or not at all).

- blues style
- hip-hop/R 'n' B style
- begins with an introduction
- synth chords
- bass line
- instrumental section
- call and response singing
- vocal **improvisations**
- male solo singer
- backing vocals
- strings
- tambourine.

2 What makes the arrangement sound different from the original?

Performing

3 Listen again to the original version of 'Stand By Me'. As you do so, follow the vocal **melody** from the score on page 61. Now sing the song as a class, carefully following the music.

Melody line of 'Stand By Me'

4 Using the original version of 'Stand By Me', examine its other textural layers:

- the bass line
- the chord sequence.

As you do so, think about the structure of the song.

Bass line to original version of 'Stand By Me'

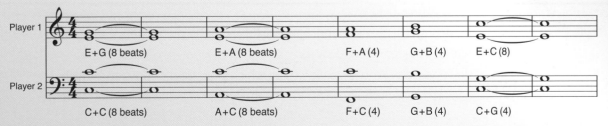

Chord sequence to original version of 'Stand By Me'

5 Working in groups of four, prepare a performance of the original version of 'Stand By Me'.

Then create your own arrangement of this version. Think about:

- a different type/style of song for your arrangement
- what features of the music you will need to adapt and refine in order to change the style of the song.

Arranging a popular song

In this lesson you will:

- create your own arrangement of a popular song based on the resources available in your group

- rehearse and perform your arrangement to the rest of your class.

During your last music lessons of Key Stage 3 you are going to work in groups to create an arrangement of a popular song. You will then perform your arrangement. You will be given three popular songs to choose from. If you do not want to perform an arrangement of a popular song suggested here, you could research your own song and use that instead.

You will need the music for the song you choose. This will give you the lyrics, chords, melody, bass line and possibly a piano arrangement of the song.

The four popular songs that have been given as suggestions are:

- 'Love is All Around' from the film *Four Weddings and a Funeral*, performed by the group Wet, Wet, Wet
- 'When You Say Nothing at All' from the film *Notting Hill*, performed by Ronan Keating
- 'Angels' written and performed by Robbie Williams
- 'Every Breath You Take' by The Police.

Producing your arrangement

Here's a suggestion on how to tackle the task.
- First, choose which song you want to work with.
- Think about how your arrangement will sound. This will be a unique performance of a popular song based on your own group's influences and styles.
- Briefly discuss your arrangement. Who is going to play which part, how and when? Which instruments are you going to use? Who is going to sing the **lyrics**? (It is a vocal performing task after all!)
- Rehearse your song and make the most use of the time available.
- Most of all, have fun and enjoy your final performance of Key Stage 3!

7th chord (p11) A chord that adds a note a flattened 7th above the root of the chord; 7th chords have a different colour to normal chords and are used a lot in jazz.

12-bar blues (p5) The name given to the chord sequence used in blues music.

a cappella (p21) Singing without instrumental accompaniment.

Abstract Art (p40) A trend in painting and sculpture in the Twentieth Century. Abstract art seeks to break away from traditional representation of physical objects. It explores the relationships of forms and colours, whereas more traditional art uses more recognizable images.

Added note chord (p12) A chord that has notes 'added' onto the notes that form the basic chord – e.g. chord of C = C, E, G; added chord of C = C, E, G + B.

Alap (p33) The first section of an Indian raga where the notes of the raga are introduced and explored in a free rhythm and with drone accompaniment.

Arranging (p56) Adapting and refining a theme/song based on the resources available.

Blues (p5) Describes the style of music originating from African-American slaves and based on a chord progression known as the 12-bar blues.

Blues scale (p9) A scale of notes used in jazz and blues music, often for solo improvisations; in the key of C, the notes of the blues scale are C, E♭, F, F#, G, B♭, C.

Boogie-woogie (p7) A style of jazz written for the piano based on the 12-bar blues chord progression and characterised by a repeated riff in the bass part (left hand).

Brass (p48) The section of the orchestra that contains trumpets, trombones, French horns and tuba.

Bugle (p47) An instrument of copper or brass, similar to the trumpet but higher in pitch and more piercing; formerly it was equipped with keys or valves, but now exists only in natural form and is used in military field music.

Chord (p5) Two or more notes played together, often to support a melody; most chords use three notes, some have four – e.g. added note and 7th chords.

Chord sequence (p5) A sequence of chords.

Chromatic scale (p21) A scale consisting of twelve semitones.

Commission (p49) A request to a composer to produce a piece of music for a particular purpose – e.g. a special occasion.

Counter melody (p56) A melody that is played or sung at the same time as the main melody.

Cyclic (p36) A melody or rhythm that is repeated over and over again.

Djembe (p36) A type of traditional African drum.

Drone (p56) A single long-held note that can be used to accompany a theme.

Duple metre (p17) Rhythms that are divided into groups of two beats are said to be in duple metre.

Equal temperament (p21) A system developed from the 16th century onwards, whereby the space between two notes an octave apart is divided into twelve equal steps.

Fanfare (p46) A short, lively, loud piece of music usually composed for brass instruments and drums; a fanfare is usually warlike or victorious in character and can be used to mark the arrival of someone important.

Gat (p33) The third section of an Indian raga where the tabla enters playing the tala rhythm and then improvises on the tala while the melody player improvises on the notes of the raga.

Harmonic series (p47) The limited range of notes played by instruments such as bugles and valveless trumpets.

Heterometres (p17) Music, or more specifically rhythms, that combine different groupings of beats (for example, duple metre and triple metre).

Homophonic texture (p50) Musical texture often called chordal, where the music can be heard in block chords.

Imitation (p47) A kind of musical copying where one musical part echoes another.

Improvised/improvisation (p9, 25, 60) A piece or a section of music that has not previously been prepared.

Jhalla (p33) The fourth and final section of an Indian raga where all instruments play together with increased tempo and a rhythmic climax.

Jor (p33) The second section of an Indian raga where the melody and drone instruments increase in tempo and play to a more steady pulse.

Key (p5, p9, 20) The key of a piece of music determines which notes are sharpened or flattened. Major and minor keys have a different pattern of tones and semitones. The number of sharps of flats in each key is called the Key Signature.

Lyrics (p22, 62) The words of a song.

Major (p13, 20) A series of notes following a certain pattern of tones and semitones; sometimes described as 'happy'.

March (p52) Music often in 2/4 time signature suitable for marching at a steady, sometimes stately, tempo.

Melody (p7, 12, 26, 43, 48, 60) Another word to describe the main tune; can be vocal or instrumental.

Meter (p25) The division of a rhythm into parts of equal time value.

Microtone (p21) An interval smaller than a semitone. Microtones are most often found in the music of cultures such as Greece, India and Japan.

Minor (p20, 50) A series of notes following a certain pattern of tones and semitones; sometimes described as 'sad'.

Modulation (p20) Changing between two tonalities, keys or scales. For example, Balkan music often modulates between major and minor scales.

Mood (p49) The atmosphere or effect created by a piece of music.

Mordent (p25) An ornament in which a note is played in rapid alternation with the note below it.

Motif (p40) A short tune or musical figure that characterizes and unifies a composition, usually only a few notes long; can be a melodic, harmonic or rhythmic pattern that is easily recognizable throughout the composition.

Ornaments (p18) Alterations to individual notes in a piece of music to add interest. Examples include trills, grace notes, glissandos and mordents.

Ostinato (p52, 56), A short repeated musical pattern sometimes called a riff; can be a rhythm or notes of a melody.

Passing note (p47) A note that appears between two other notes in stepwise motion.

Phase in/out (p43) The gradual introduction or termination of a new rhythmic or melodic idea introduced into the texture of Minimalist music.

Pitch (p47) The highness or lowness of a sound.

Polyrhythms (p36) The use of several rhythms performed simultaneously, often overlapping each other to create a thick texture.

Primary chords (p5) Chords I, IV and V in any key; these chords are used to play the 12-bar blues and many other kinds of music.

Pulse (p25) The regular beat of a piece of music.

Raga (31) A group of notes rather like a melody on which Indian music is based; 'raga' is also used to describe the actual 'piece' of Indian music.

Riff (p7) A short repeating pattern of notes sometimes called an ostinato.

Root (p11) The note on which a chord is based – e.g. the chord of C would have C as its root.

Round (p56) A song in which different performers sing the same tune starting one after the other, similar to a canon.

Rubato (p25) A term used to describe slightly speeding up or slowing down the tempo of a piece or a section of music at the discretion of the solo player.

Semitone (p21) The smallest distance in Western music between two notes – e.g. C to C# or E to F.

Swing (p7) A type/style of rhythm used in jazz and blues music.

Tanpura (p30) A type of stringed instrument found in different versions in different places around the world; most are types of plucked lutes.

Ternary (p51) A three-part musical structure – A B A – where A is repeated at the beginning and end of a piece with a contrasting section in the middle.

Theme (p56) A musical idea, usually the main tune or melody.

Toccata (p25) Music written to show off the skills of the performer, usually for the organ or another keyboard instrument ,and with lots of fast and difficult scale passages and improvised and organised sections.

Tonality (p20) The relationship between notes of different pitches in a musical scale.

Trill (p7, 26, 52) A rapid alternation of two adjacent notes, often called a Shake.

Triple metre (p17) Rhythms that are divided into groups of three beats are said to be in triple metre.

Variation (p56) Where a theme is altered or changed musically while still retaining features of the original theme.

Walking bass line (p6) A bass line based on the notes of a chord, often with added notes, that 'walks' up and down between the notes like the movement of the bass player's fingers.